At the Edge of the Cliff

poems

Marian Kaplun Shapiro

A book of poetry and drawings that explore emotional disconnections, silences, and efforts to make contact. ...her purpose is to pursue "extremes of feeling" and their resulting epiphanies through "experimenting with form and content." These experiments encompass diagrams, sketches, spacing, and unusual typography, which often focus attention on conceptual organization. ...Poems that creatively reveal the unsaid and unsayable.
—*Kirkus Reviews*

Complete review online on *Kirkus Review* website:
https://www.kirkusreviews.com/book-reviews/marian-kaplun-shapiro/at-the-edge-of-the-cliff-poems/

At the Edge of the Cliff

poems

Marian Kaplun Shapiro

Plain View Press, LLC
1101 W 34th Street, STE 404

www.plainviewpress.net
Austin, TX 78705

Copyright © 2021 Marian Kaplun Shapiro. All rights reserved under International and Pan-American Copyright Conventions. No part of this book may be reproduced or distributed in any form or by any means, or stored in a data base or retrieval system, without written permission from the author. All rights, including electronic, are reserved by the author and publisher.

ISBN: 978-1-63210-083-2
Library of Congress Control Number: 2020949222

Digital Artist: David Shapiro
Cover art: "Drifting Leaves" painting by Patricia C.K. Macintyre
Cover design by Pam Knight

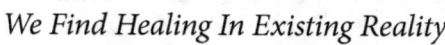

We Find Healing In Existing Reality
Plain View Press is a 40-year-old issue-based literary publishing house. Our books result from artistic collaboration between writers, artists, and editors. Over the years we have become a far-flung community of humane and highly creative activists whose energies bring humanitarian enlightenment and hope to individuals and communities grappling with the major issues of our time—peace, justice, the environment, education and gender.

To my loving husband Irwin Shapiro.

As an astrophysicist, his is the world of outer space. Mine is focused on the inner world. Yet we met on earth, and in less than two weeks knew we wanted to spend our lives together. That was over 60 years ago. I've learned a little science from him, and he a lot of poetry from one particular author. It's been and remains quite a partnership.

Contents

Introduction   11
Experiment   12

Part 1: What Time Is It?   13

Table of Contents: A Map   13
What We Know   15
Over Your Head   16
Plane Geometry   17
Same old   18
Summer's   19
Blow Up   20
John Cage in the Wild   21
The news   22
Quaker Meeting on the Concord River   23
Clocks   24
3 a.m.   25
Yet   (again)   26
Coinage   27
Stonehenge   28
Gardening   29
Pinwheel of Life   30
Tree/Winter, Figure/Ground   31
Nexus   32
Bird calls   33

Part 2: Dividing Line   35

Memoir   37
Rape   38
Dividing Line   39
You're Still Hung Up on Something That Happened
    Fifty Years Ago?   40
Chorus   42
Prayer After....   43

Ellipses	44
Wednesday, During the Hurricane	45
Repetitive Nightmare	46
Late Night Flight	47
Instructions to Child Victims of Torture Regarding Training for the Future Commission of a Massacre	49
Mayday	50
Speaking Up	51
(no longer a) Simple Decision	52
Internal Monologue	53

Part 3: The Edge of the Cliff   (If Not Now, When?)   55

Empathy	57
Monkey Mind	58
Crescendo, Decrescendo, Sostenuto	59
Cryopediology	60
Mixed Message	61
In Words of One Syllable	62
Unspoken	63
Before (The) After (Quaker Meeting)	64
Mobile	65
Christmas Oratorio	66
A New Song	67
Please Submit a Brief Bio	68
Calling	69
Spring Sunlight	70
Synesthesia	71
Auld Lang Syne	72
Deciding	73
Cartography	74
"If Not Now, When?"	75
Pure Love	76
Non-Sense	77
Editing It Down	78
One way or another	79

'Across the Miles'	80
Breakfast, Together	81
Wind Advisory	82
Modern Haiku (while aggravated)	83
Getting to the Point	84
Fauré Requiem: Les Fenêtres de Ste Chapelle, 18h30	85
Living Together	87
Suburban Back Yard	88
Before the Memorial Day Weekend	89
Pain. Hope.	90
Learning from Bees	91
Echolalia, in September	92
Bereavement Group	93
Internet Search	94
Equation: A Conversation	95
Weathering the War of Words	96
Communication	97
Hearing/Not Hearing in the Conference Hall	98
Anxious Attachment	99
Assembly	100
Right Triangles	101
Behind You There Is Nothing	102
Around here, March	103
Life Lessons	105
Experiments in	106
Climbing	107
Acknowledgements	109
About the Author	111

Introduction

As you climb, the path twists and turns, but makes its way upward, determined and indefatigable. All of the tributaries matter. All of the flowers, the weeds, the brambles and mossy muddy byways are essential to the landscape. Please take your time to look around. Stop when you get tired; stop when you want to think, absorb, respond....

Writing has always been an experiment for me. Breaking the rules means knowing the rules—even the unspoken rules about structure—what IS a poem?—but also, even what topics are suitable for poetry—how about rape? Bombs? Torture? Well, why not?

WHY NOT is one question. Another, however, is WHY. Not just to be 'different.' These poems do not abandon form, although they rarely look like the forms you learned in high school. To write against these structured forms is to respect and honor them by moving in directions that don't work for you now. Atonal music does not reject the diatonic scale. The computer does not reject the typewriter or the pen, or the quill. But it cannot help but come from this author in this century. And too, this reader. For you and me, it is experimental. For someone not yet born, perhaps not.

Although some poems look 'traditional'—lines that scan, a metaphor, perhaps even an end rhyme—there's probably something else meant to surprise, to startle, even to shock. Sound, position, font, synesthesia, neologisms, punctuation...all can disrupt our fundamental givens. The organizing principle by which I write is the same as the one that underlies that life trajectory and my work as a psychologist: The unconscious is the place in each of us from which our deepest self-learning (and therefore our possibilities for empathy) spring. We can't see it for ourselves, of course—But when we let our guard down—it has a chance to come into the air. Notice the use of space in these poems—as in music—the place for you to listen to yourself. That space, when partnered with surprise, punctures our protective layer, becoming more possible to open our human, mostly-closed minds, and find the center that we yearn for.

And especially, there are the drawings, seeds of which showed up back in my twenties, which, en route to my eighties, began to overtake the words themselves. Integrating words and images gave me a way in which to work in layers of time and feeling, as my life extended into another phase. Many of these highly visual poems address the extremes of feeling—from love and peace to their twinned shadows of the horrors of which human beings seem endlessly capable. All part of life, and therefore of poetry, along with nature, beauty, joy, grief, and the need to face one's own mortality.

Some people pursue this state of epiphany through mood altering drugs, and other ecstatic experiences—religion, music, extreme sports...I pursue it here through poetry. That is the purpose of my experimenting with form and content. Every poem in this collection is an experiment. Welcome to your climb.

Experiment

To experiment is
to live on
the edge of a   cliff

to toss your parachute
into the down-
draught. To leave yourself
no escape.

Make your home there
for as long as
you can bear it. Or
learn to love its
wild
solitude.

Part 1:
What Time Is It?

In this first section I invite you into my experience, and into your experience, asking you as I have asked myself: Why here? Where are we going? What time is it? What is foreground? background? These questions move us into the future, pulling on the past, landing in the present.

Which instantly—is gone.

Table of Contents: A Map

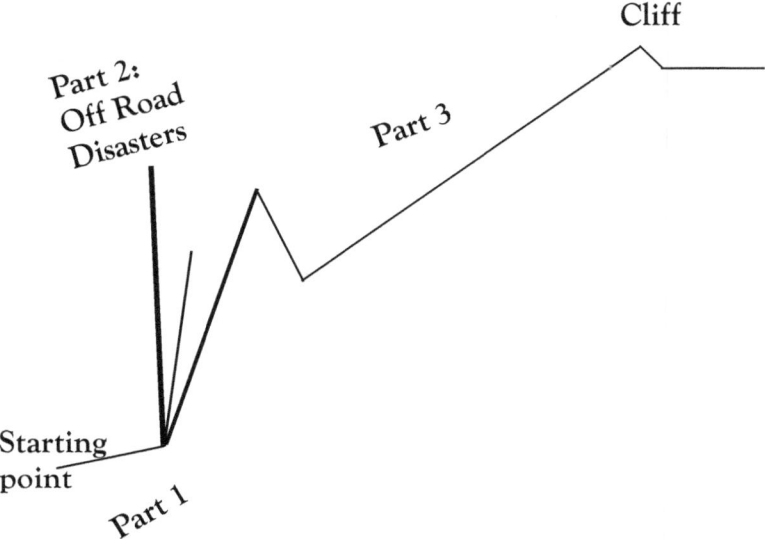

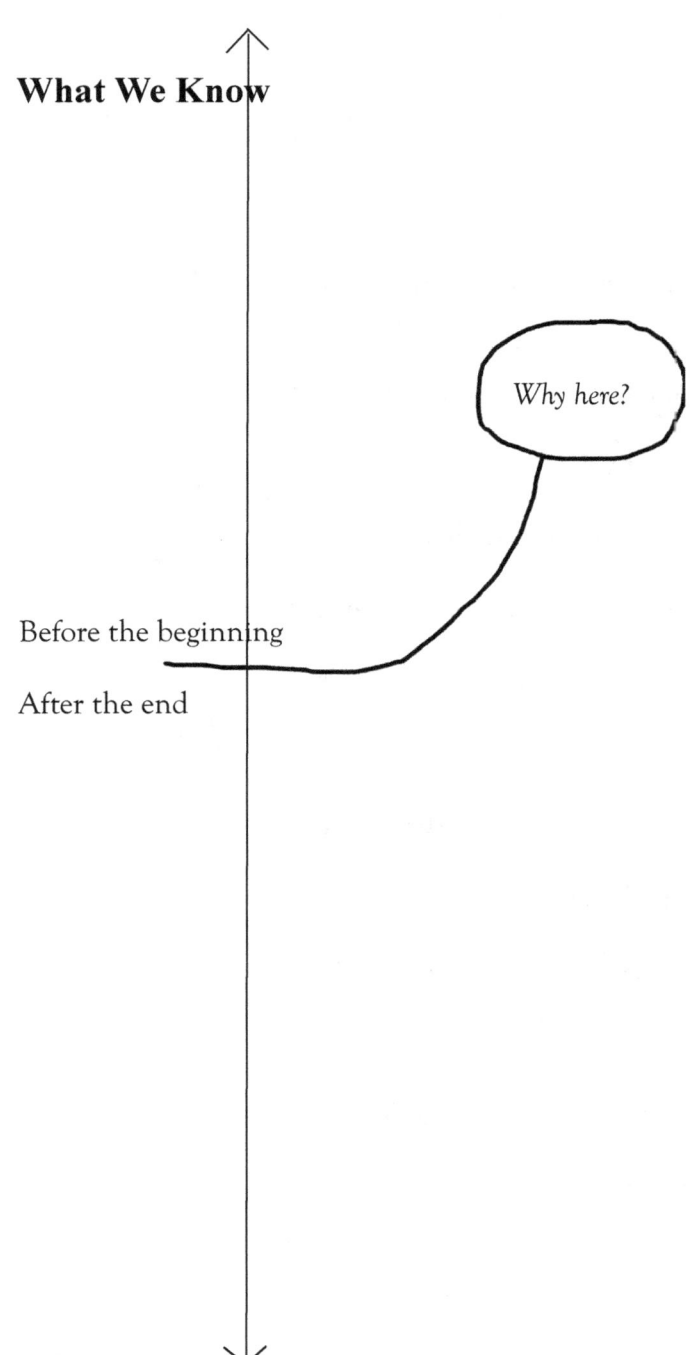

Over Your Head

Before you learn to swim

    remember that you are not a fish

    or a turtle, or even a dog, or a duck

Don't go over your head

    even with your water wings

        firmly hugging you, and be sure

the lifeguard is paying attention to *you*

    (not to that cell phone or that cute kid

        showing off in the shallow end).

Sometimes it's good to be afraid

    of riptides and undertows, of lightning

        and hurricanes. Of jellyfish and sharks.

It will be many years before you know

    when you are safe

    to be out of your depth.

Plane Geometry

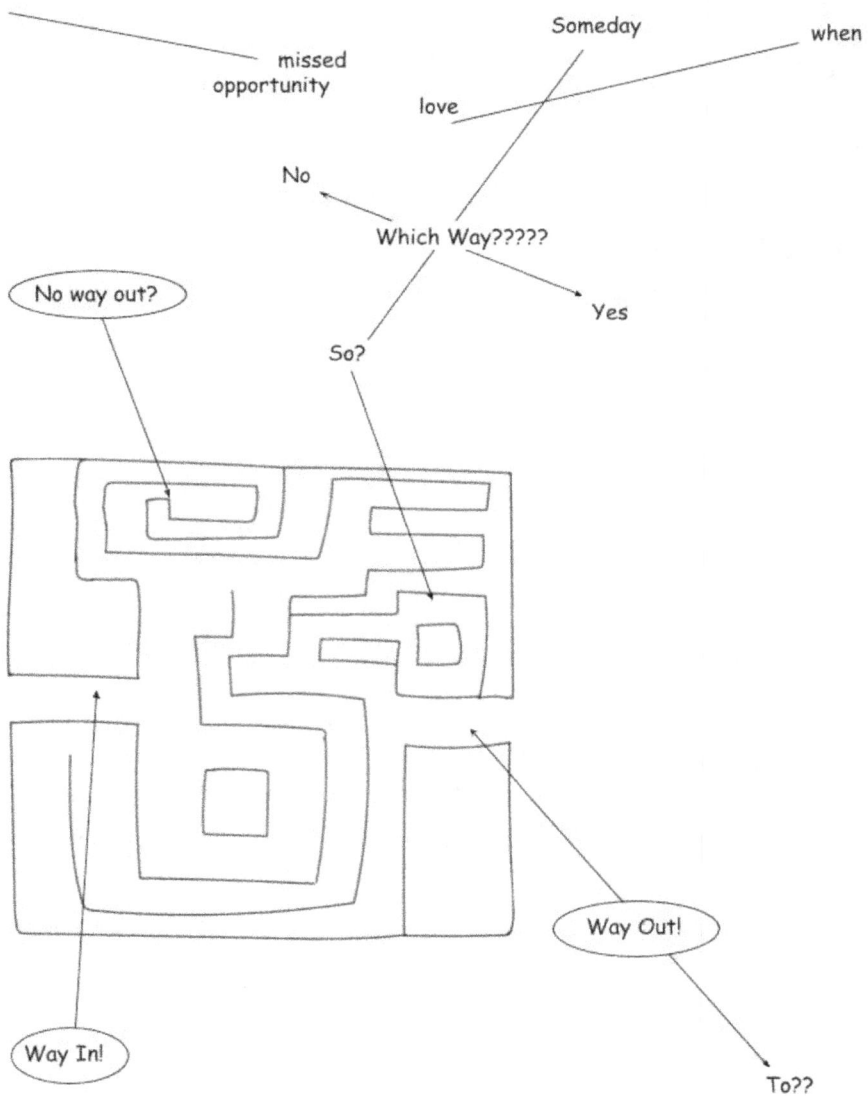

Same old

cabin on (the
lake)
birches by (the
lake)
duck swimming in (the
lake)
us paddling across (the
lake)
eating strawberry
       pie on the
       porch
       overlooking
       the

.... lake lake lake lake lake lake lake lake lake lake lake lake
lake lake lake lake lake lake lake lake lake lake lake lake lake lake lake lake
lake lake lake lake lake lake lake lake lake lake lake ....

Night. A storm is coming up. Thunder from the south, across the water. Same old lightning stunning the

same old

sky

Summer's

sweet
smell of star   clang
of sun-
rise   riddle of lilypads
a yesness of raspberry pie. Topaz

moon rising. Inch
by stellar inch we learn why
we need horizon: To weigh

the whatness of lake
the whoness of mountain

the whenness of
sky.

Blow Up

Let's blow up all the sentences, let's blow up all the lines, the words the syllables the letters,

make them sooooooooooo big they are practically screaming to be ssshhhatterrrred dd to s m
  i t
     her
               ee
               ns

let's bomb them all until we find the center, the nut, the pit, the nougat inside the screaming, the deepest silence ever heard, the core of all of it. Start there.

John Cage in the Wild

Silence.

What   about   the   rabbit?

Her ears at attention, she

waits.   Silence.

Listens.   Silence.

Waits.   Hears

the sound

of her breathing.

The music of

our breath.

The news

is sailing crackling past us at supersonic speed, he said this she said
that, this that this that the polls are swaying the babies are crying the
mothersfathers are shushing, the gun owners shouting the teapot is
screaming the slot machines pinging (the house is winning)
the storm is threatening thundering diminishing leaving gone
the drought is over (for the time being) the sparrow is singing (such
a beautiful song, that little brown bird) the chainsaw is screeching,
the leafblower roaring and somewhere all is quiet>quieter>quieter
where is that place?

Quaker Meeting on the Concord River

```
Paddles slapslapping

            box turtle splashes, startled

   by us              deer sweeping across thistled

       field                              silence


                blueblack dragonfly      cloudwisps


silence                      of           heron

    sipping at marshside   stretching  sipping

    sipping                              stretching


              silence silence                    all

       the way to the hollow      where the ducks

  are resting                     where

  geese V-form overhead                   white

              silence         silence

  you and I            sky              wind


       air
```

Clocks

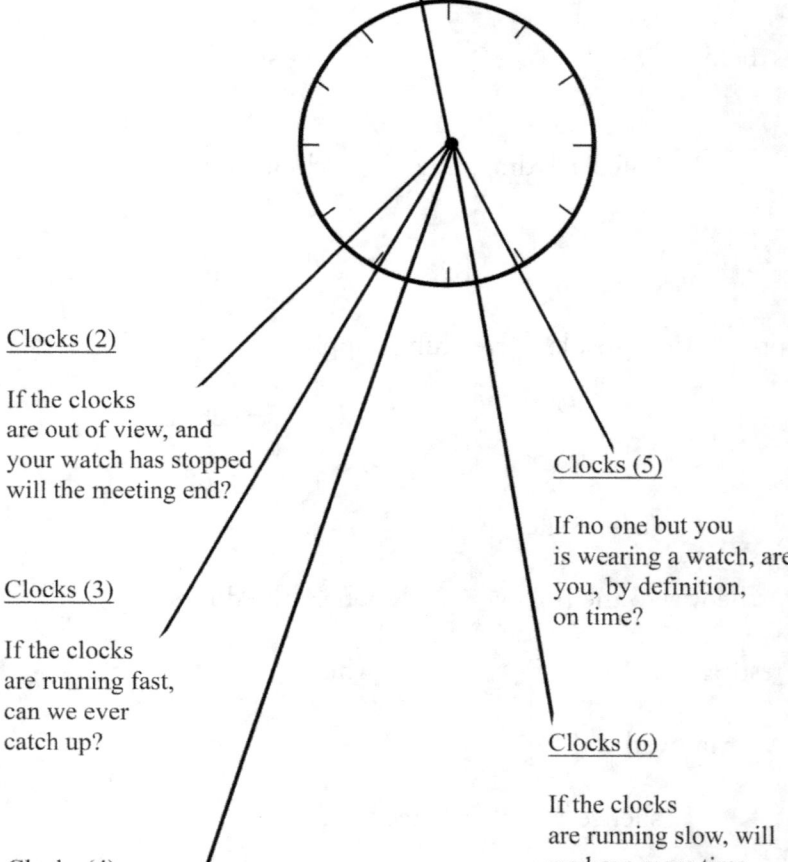

Clocks (1)

If the clocks
had stopped, and
you aren't wearing a watch,
what time is it?

Clocks (2)

If the clocks
are out of view, and
your watch has stopped
will the meeting end?

Clocks (3)

If the clocks
are running fast,
can we ever
catch up?

Clocks (4)

If no one but you
is wearing a watch, can
you be late?

or early?

Clocks (5)

If no one but you
is wearing a watch, are
you, by definition,
on time?

Clocks (6)

If the clocks
are running slow, will
we have more time
than we thought?

3 a.m.

— suddenly a little flame escapes from the rock. Smoke slides upward towards the moon as she dances backward, an old-fashioned waltz across the glittering ballroom floor. *One* two three, *turn* two three. *Glide* two three. *Dip* two three. *Will you won't you will you won't you, will you join the dance?* O how she yearns to follow. Grab on! the mock turtle croaks, encouragingly. It's only now once.

Yet   (again)

                long trip   (from somewhere)   thankgod
                        home at last   mail
piled   up   on   kitchen
table/chairs   stacks of bills   coupons   (expired)
      flyers   catalogues   pleas, scams, Lancôme
specials department store sales (three days only)   bank
    statements   weeks of
newspapersmagazinesjournals rejectionletterslettersletters   (nonono)
    (*although we do hope you'll send your work next year*)   *Didn't you sleep
on the plane?* (husband asks, having slept)
                            Sleeping on the plane isn't sleeping
(*the captain has turned on the seat belt sign*)
                (*we are now at 32,000 feet*)   hungry
neck   hurts   bored   thirsty   (*how long
   until we land*)   (*dreaming of bed*)   Dreaming
  of my bed   But now

        I notice that my bicycle has disappeared
        from the front porch   (I wouldn't leave
        it there)   (I haven't ridden it in many
        years)   way in the distance
        I see a neighbor's son or daughter—
        too far to tell exactly who—doing wheelies. It's
        my bike!   My bike!   my husband
        materializes in the doorway, telling me
        not to worry about it, calm down,
        give it up, I'm too old to ride a bike
        anyway, let the neighborhood kids enjoy it. I'm
        so tired   so tired   But a strong wind
        lifts me, blowing me up the street. *I want
        my bike back!* I shout. *It's my bike, and
        I want to ride it!*

Coinage

& what about *small* change
not revelation/born-again size,
not learned-my-lesson size.
I'm talking pennies.
I'm talking nickels and dimes. Still,
when you've saved a whole jar full,
they're worth more than the dollar bills
the bank will trade them in for.

Stonehenge

Suppose nothing
could be changed, no
stones rearranged
nothing
broken
nothing
needing repair
where
would I be then? and you?

Gardening

    (a haibun)

One year we said let's try something new, the fiery poppy, the joyous sunflower—but nothing could convince them to make do with shade, and the shade will be here forever unless we cut down all the giant oaks to which I say Absolutely Not!

pinwheel of life   spin
us around   seeking brilliance
finding something else

Pinwheel of Life

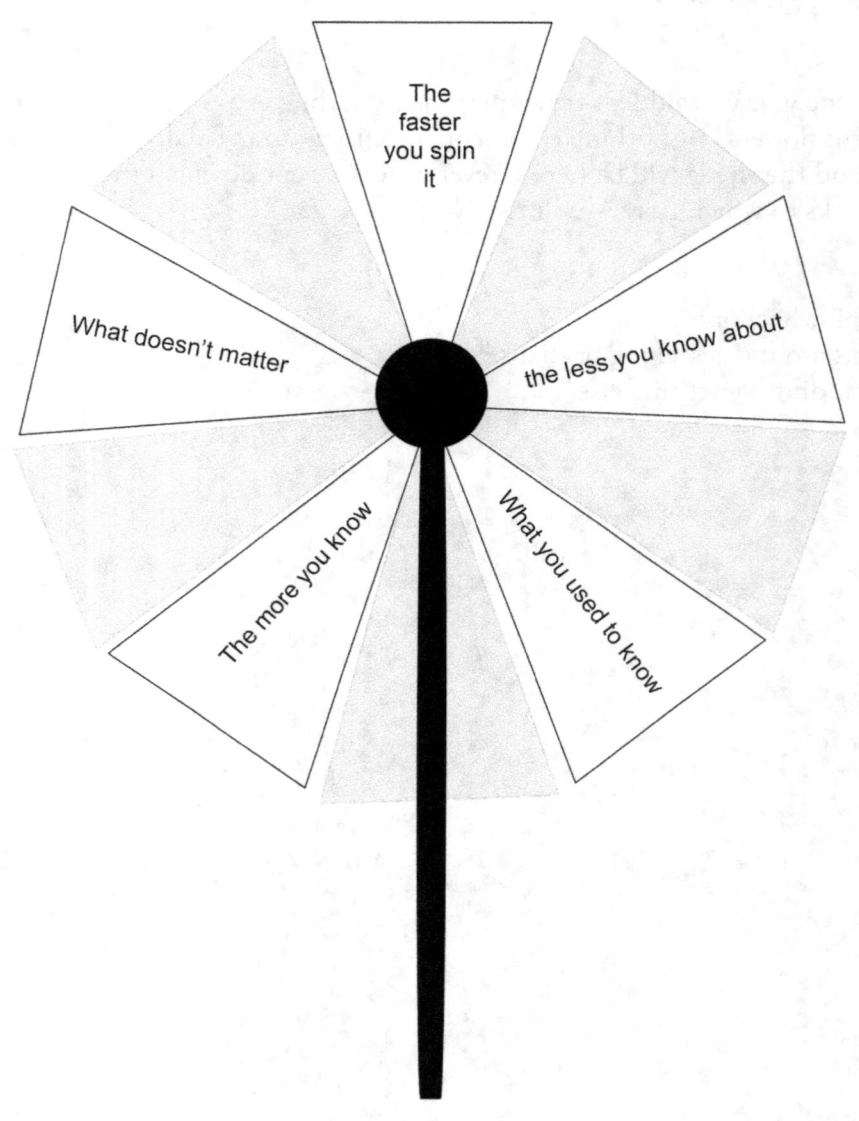

Tree/Winter, Figure/Ground

Bran   ches
            bent
      bare

      bro-
ken   an/gles naked

                ge-

ometry

Reverse ground, artist!

Winter/Trees

Amazing the Light!

Nexus

Some day I'm going to take off without permission, an elevator gone rogue, rising higher, higher through the roof the air traffic controllers bored anxious velcroed to their desks in their airless offices in their airless air terminals in their airless air while I become a red-tailed hawk, a loon, a goose, a sparrow singing swooping landing here, there, a pink balloon a yellow kite, a summer hat, an autumn leaf, a seed, a prayer, an answer, another question

Bird calls

are
     air-bubbling
          all   around us   from   green   of   trees
     bushes
        curving beak of   great   blue   heron posing one-
leggèd on a rock   by the turtles' enclave on the bank
    of the river,   over the turnpike   flying in formation,
                         vees on the way to elsewhere
  yodeling into the dark, calling for their mates   across the lake
       on the window
   sill, coo-cooing their big-city song hoo-hooing   cock-a-doodle
doo-ing,   shrieking   quacking caw-cawing chick-a-dee-dee-deeing
     trilling,   singing the what-cheer-cheer-cheer,   the tut-tut-tut,
        the whirrr...

        And here we are. Looking through
        our spyglasses. Listening. We try
        to call to them, twisting our lips
        and tongues every which way, but
        they know we aren't for real. Human
        is what we are. Birds are what
        they are. All of us, singing.
        All of us lovers, children, parents,
        friends. Hearing each other
        when we can.

Part 2:
Dividing Line

The before.　　　　　　The after. The biggest space one can—and can't—imagine. Between when all is (kinda) all right. When nothing is. Such a moment may be memorialized in the headlines: 911. Or may be known by no one but you. Alone in that knowledge, you find a way to go on:

REMEMBER to forget, every day.
FORGET to remember you forgot.

　　　　—Instructions to Child Victims of Torture

Memoir

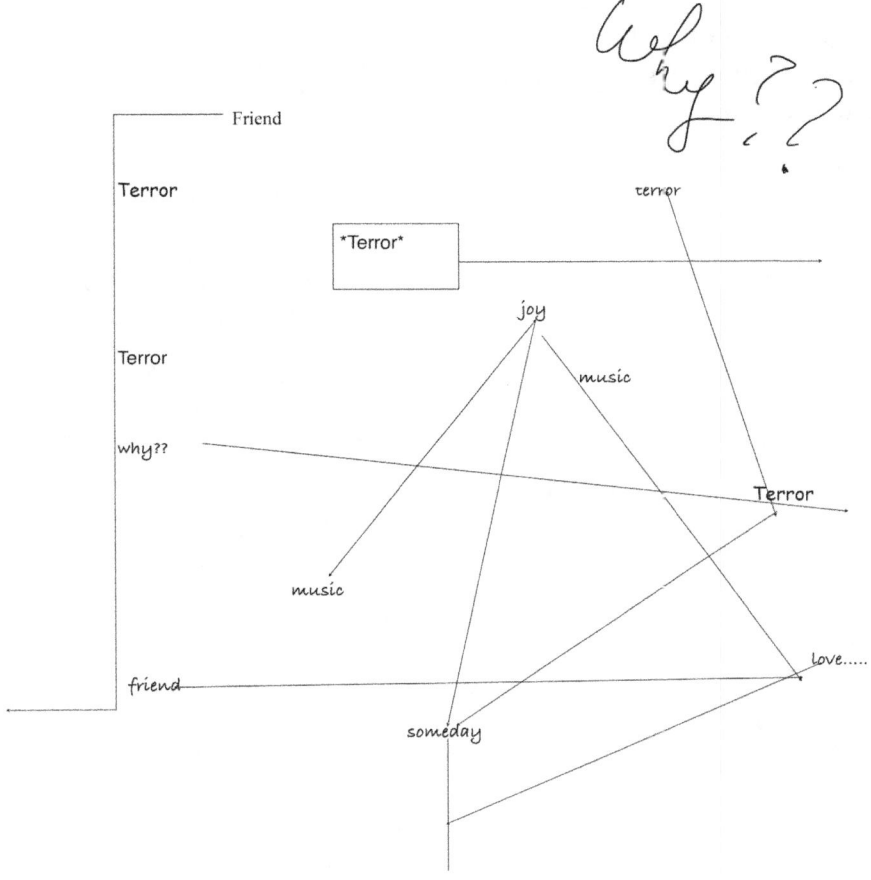

Rape

(a senyru)

That day in pink shorts
(subway singing, sun smiling)
No one knew I'd died.

Dividing Line

10:45

Pink shorts, ironed carefully. Her shirt a field of linen blooming with violets. Moon-lit by five tiny silver buttons. She adds a purple ribbon to her ponytail, clutched high in a rubber band. A few tendrils wisping by.

A day to fry eggs on the sidewalk, as New Yorkers say.

Fourth of July. Macy's closed. Gristedes closed. Down by the subway, the news stand's always open. Good day for a pepsi. Guys ragging on each other. Working their smoke rings. Playing their lucky numbers.

Swings lifeless. Benches vacant. The big kids hanging at Orchard Beach. Their little sisters off to girlscout camp. The Catskills for a week, sleeping in tents, whacking mosquitoes.

She's thinking of an ice cream. Later, maybe Loews for a movie. What's on today? Doesn't matter. Air-conditioned heaven.

NOON ──────────────────────────────

1:00

Shorts. The once-pink of them makes her nauseous. Ripped waistband. Hair glued to sweat-streaked neck. Ribbon long gone. Shirt a soggy dishrag headed for the trash. Four silver buttons. One hole.

A day to fry eggs on the sidewalk. A Fourth of July to remember. A taste like wet nickels. I hate you, she'd said. She knew what that meant.

You're Still Hung Up on Something That Happened Fifty Years Ago?

Having survived
        having survived and
                more important
                        having lived through all those years

having lived through all those years, minutes, hours, days, days without end, days with endless days in front of them, in back of them, having lived through living through the consequences, the immediate consequences and the consequences directly connected and the consequences indirectly connected and the consequences connected in ways no one else could conjure up (how come you wouldn't touch vanilla icecream with a tenfootpole, as they say, for example, although no one knows or even notices that you choose every flavor but), now someone says to you (eyebrow aloft) *you're still hung up on something that happened fifty years ago?* And by that they mean that they don't want to hear about it, they don't want to hear how it defined you, how it weighed in when you chose to marry and whom you chose to marry, that weighed in whispering from the prompter's box more often than even you have known. That, in fact, it weighed something. That it counted. That it counts.

Forget it, they say. *Forgive and forget. It's water under the bridge.*

Well, that takes care of it. After the package is finally sliced open using the biggest scissors that you own, you'll rip the box into manageable pieces for recycling. The cardboard sides in one bin, the brown paper wrapping crumpled separately, the styrofoam sticking to the plastic takeout trays, rinsed and segregated as required by Waste Management. And what of the contents of the carton? Nod pleasantly as if you aren't disappointed, as if you aren't horrified, as if you're not repulsed, revolted. Later, when the others take their leave, thanking you for a lovely party while reclaiming their coatshatsscarvespocketbooks from entombment in the bed in the

once-kid's now spare room, you can dispose of it, burying it in
the garbage can between the corn cobs and the turkey bones that
shouldn't make their way down the cantankerous disposal. The best
you can hope for is a future in the landfill, aka the old town dump.
The compost of your life. Its next incarnation.

Yes, remembering
        isn't optional. Who is it
                who's remembering?
                      You with the great life?

It's you, yes, although it's not her face that meets you in the
bedroom mirror. It's you, yes, you with the braids, you with the high
voice, you with the little legs that runrunrun around the bases, that
skip, that jump, that win the hopping contest. It's you polkadotted
with measles. It's you counting on your fingers, you changing the
ribbon on dad's (your) old Royal, ink all over your fingers. It's you
opening your diary with the little gold key, you writing *Hot day. Went
swimming*. You being careful, you knowing that your secrets aren't
safe on paper, you pretending you don't know it's just a pretend
lock. It's you promising not to tell, crossyourheartandhopetodie.
Back then was long ago. Far away. Sometimes it seems she was
another girl, from another country with another language. You
aren't bothered by the memory of barking dogs any more. When you
hear them, you remember that you know how to let sleeping dogs
lie. And, in the worst case scenario, how to run like hell.

Chorus

because   why

        the reason is

   isn't

that   or

     therefore
forget it
never mind
put it behind you
what's done is done
suck it up
rise above it
Hey!
Life goes on!

Prayer After….

Thank you God
for every minute
when things aren't
worse.

Ellipses

      you know how it is...
              because, after all...   considering...
well, of course...   ...in those days
    not that he meant anything by it...
        better to forgive and forget...
...of course, of course...   it's water under the bridge...
    ...it was a shame...   if only he...
        we don't like to say...
      ...not right, though   I didn't know...
...too late   too late...
        ...to do anything anyway.

Wednesday, During the Hurricane

The leaves are singing
    the birds are falling
the rain is rising
        the sky is aching
(worms laughing)
(apples dancing)

Wednesday is weeping.
The trees are waltzing
in place,   waiting
patiently.   The moon
floats barefoot.
Tuesday remembers
flipflops. Sand between toes.
Thursday remembers
the
death
march,
the
naked
snow

Repetitive Nightmare

I've lost my pocketbook

Please help me!

my voice won't work

Help! Help!

the phone is dead

Loss *Betrayal* *Terror* *Violence* *Rape*

The wolves. The hyenas. The jackals. They
wait patiently. Hungrily. They are not
your neighbor's poodles that lick your hand.
Nor your auntie's kitties purring on her lap.
Nor pigeons at your toddler's playground
pecking at the cookie crumbs.

The mares of night are out to kill you.
And you know it.

Late Night Flight

*Flight 3099 to Where You're Going is delayed
until 9 o'clock.* DO NOT LEAVE BAGGAGE
AND PARCELS UNATTENDED. I need coffee.
A bagel. ATTENTION! THIS IS A PUBLIC
SERVICE ANNOUNCEMENT! CARDIAC
DEFIBRILLATORS ARE AVAILABLE
THROUGHOUT THE AIRPORT. A young
man reads his little boy a cow-shaped picture
book, mooing every so often. "More, daddy,"
begs the child. Daddy complies. ATTENTION!
THIS AIRPORT IS SMOKE-FREE. ALL PETS
MUST BE IN CARRIERS. IN AN EMERGENCY
DIAL 911. Two rubber plants stand green guard
by the automatic doors, laconic Mutt and Jeffs.

*Flight 8915 to Somewhere Else is oversold. We are
looking for two volunteers to give up their seats.*
ALL PETS MUST BE IN CARRIERS. You're out
of cream? You call that a <u>bagel</u>? IN AN EMERGENCY
DIAL 911. ATTENTION! THIS AIRPORT IS SMOKE-
FREE. *We will not be going to Somewhere Else if we
don't get two volunteers!* ALL PETS MUST BE IN
CARRIERS. *Attention, passengers! Flight 3099 is now
scheduled to depart at 10:45. Flight 8915 is boarding at
gate 12.* The toddler's mood is fraying."Bye bye, plane,"
daddy offers hopefully, pointing out and up. "Horsie!
Horsie!" toddler escalates, pulling Daddy's belt. Daddy's
coffee spills. Daddy is fraying. DO NOT LEAVE
BAGGAGE AND PARCELS UNATTENDED. Fuck
you! *Flight 3099 is cancelled.* IN AN EMERGENCY
DIAL 911. *Please hold. All operators are currently
serving other customers. Thank you for your patience.
Please hold. Please continue to hold. During peak
hours the next available operator does not speak
English/is otherwise occupied/ will disconnect you.
The next available operator is your mother.* My

mother, once dead, has shown up for her therapy appointment. She's over by the Au Bon Pain, balancing a takeout decaf and her bag of invisible bloody knives. I've agreed to treat her since no one else will. "So pretty lady, so nice lady!" says the Asian immigrant on her minimum wage shift. "That's why nobody will treat her," I explain. "Nothing's wrong with her, all things considered." Rubber plants, teach me how you do it. CARDIAC DEFIBRILLATORS ARE AVAILABLE THROUGHOUT THE AIRPORT. DO NOT LEAVE BAGGAGE AND PARCELS UNATTENDED. Airplanes have smashed us in New York, Pennsylvania, Washington. Aid workers are beheaded by barbarians. "Abusive and degrading treatment" is not torture: "Interrogation operations were safe. secure, and humane," according to an Air Force Lt. General. ATTENTION! ALL PETS MUST BE IN CARRIERS. Arab children blow themselves up. Their parents declare them martyrs. We play taps for our dead soldiers, pin medals on those who weep. THIS IS A PUBLIC SERVICE ANNOUNCEMENT. IN AN EMERGENCY CALL 911. Rubber plants, teach me to stand upright, leaning slightly towards the sun, year after endless year.

Instructions to Child Victims of Torture Regarding Training for the Future Commission of a Massacre*

I. **FORGET** what you must not remember.
   A. *Erase your feelings.* Experiment until you find the best approach for you. Popular methods include
      1. <u>*On-off techniques:*</u> Become
         a. a light switch
         b. a water faucet
      2. <u>*Total object technique:*</u> Turn into
         a. wood
         b. stone
         c. steel
   B. *Pretend*
      1. <u>*Act normal*</u>
      2. <u>*Be pleasant if possible. (If not, be quiet.)*</u>
   C. *Prepare: Your time will come.*

II. **REMEMBER** to forget, every day.

III. **FORGET** to remember you forgot.

IV. **MAKE LISTS.**

V. **PREPARE QUIETLY.**

VI. **WAIT.**

---

*As an interesting note, this poem was composed between 1990 and 1996, long before September 11.

Mayday*

They're falling
falling clusters
clusterbombs   feathers
feathers   blood   ducks dropping
dropping   dead   shot
shot mid-air
mid-air blood showers
showers   hail
hailstones   blood
blood-streaked stones felled to earth
earthquake   flood   fire
fire   pyre   crematorium
crematorium   where you
you mother father
fathermother of you
you friend   wife   husband   dead
dead on these pages
pages of children pages
pages pictures poems
poems   pages   remembrances
remembrances of the fallen
fallen, all fallen
fallen all.

* The etymology of Mayday is from the French, "M'AIDER" or M'AIDEZ", namely, "help me".

Speaking Up

Why bother —
someone else will do it.

(no longer a) Simple Decision

if

why

how

where

so...

Maybe

then

Are you sure??

Internal Monologue

what if *why not* OH NONONO!
but

Forget it! *can't*
besides which SO WHAT! WHO
SCREW THAT!

I'M! (NOT) GONNA

                         DO IT!

Part 3:
The Edge of the Cliff
(If Not Now, When?)

Section 3, the longest section of this book, honors 'ordinary' life, life without terror, that daily life, its pleasures and frustrations, even its pain. I revel in the pleasures of living and treat the worst of it as best I can. Fear sits quietly in the background, no longer yelling at me from close up in loud emergency sirens. Once I valued the diamond of my unbreakable will; now I can afford to value the spirit of the "incandescent pearl" (Experiments in). What a miracle!

This section features a few of my auditory and rhythmic experiments (Spring Sunlight, for example), and many of my recent visual works, which have become the given more than the exception. As in my long life, my work as a psychologist illuminates the dark avenue that relationships can take (Unspoken; In Words Of One Syllable; Mixed Message); I feel especially blessed to have sustained a route paved with friendship and empathy. Many of these poems paint waystations of a marriage of over 60 years, the steadfast love of my husband, and of my children, grandchildren, and friends. Our canoe trips. Our rented cabin in Maine with all our family nearby. Our annual honeymoons to Paris. The flip side is loss, however, which is surely coming faster every day.

But now always I own my voice by which to share my feelings, whatever they are, and I don't need to pretend otherwise.

Hillel famously asked, "If not now, when?" I am at WHEN. Actually, we are all at 'when,' when we realize it. That is my edge of the cliff. The view is truly great from here.

──────── **Empathy**

(an architectural explication)

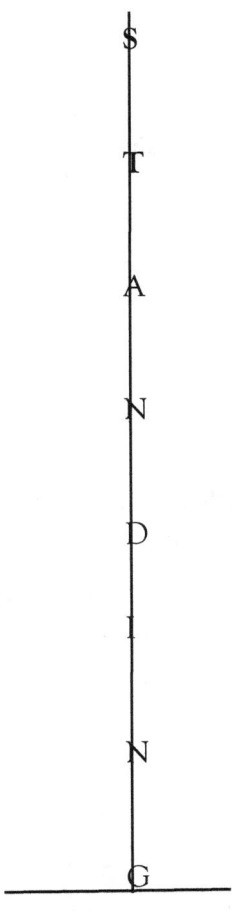

UNDER–

Monkey Mind

      rising
          falling
              rising   wedding
                  falling
        later   *rising*   e-mail
                falling
                      rising
  what if   *falling*   *rising*   rain
             rising
         falling
       rising   lunch
  falling
      rising
        falling
          rising
yesterday   *falling*
              rising
                falling
                  rising
                  falling
    once   *rising*
            falling
       rising
    falling
rising
    falling
      rising   maybe
        falling
         rising
          falling
        rising
      falling
     rising
    falling
   rising
 falling

Crescendo, Decrescendo, Sostenuto

Prayer: Allowing the light to carry us into someone else's darkness
—Gil Johnston, 7/01, Cambridge Friends Meeting

allowing the light to carry us into someone else's darkness

allowing the light to carry us into someone else's darkness

Allowing the light to carry us into someone else's darkness

Cryopediology

August.   *Showers. Thunderstorms.*

Sweat. Little worms trickled through her pores, making their homes below her skin. In one voice the cool boutiques declared bikinis over. Shorts and sandals going. Half off!

September.   *Sun or hurricane. Both.*

Bonne rentrée, as they say in Paris, kissing on both cheeks. A new start. New school outfits, freshly pressed. New pens. New notebooks. New shoes.

She loved him, she loved him, she loved him not.

The short-sleeved cotton shrugs. The long-sleeved silks. The cashmeres. V-necks. Turtles. Soupçons of autumn colors layered artfully.

She loved him, she loved him not.

October.   *Fog.*

Leaves crisping underfoot. Mannequins draped seductively in swirls of scarves. Shawls. Flinging their plastic arms from capes. Leather jackets.

She loved him not. She loved him. Not a lot.

November.   *Rain. More rain.*

Wool. Down. Sheepskin. Furs!

December.   *Ice. Snow.*

And mittens!

She told him what was what.

She loved him Not.

Mixed Message

Of course I love you   (BUT...)
It just isn't working out

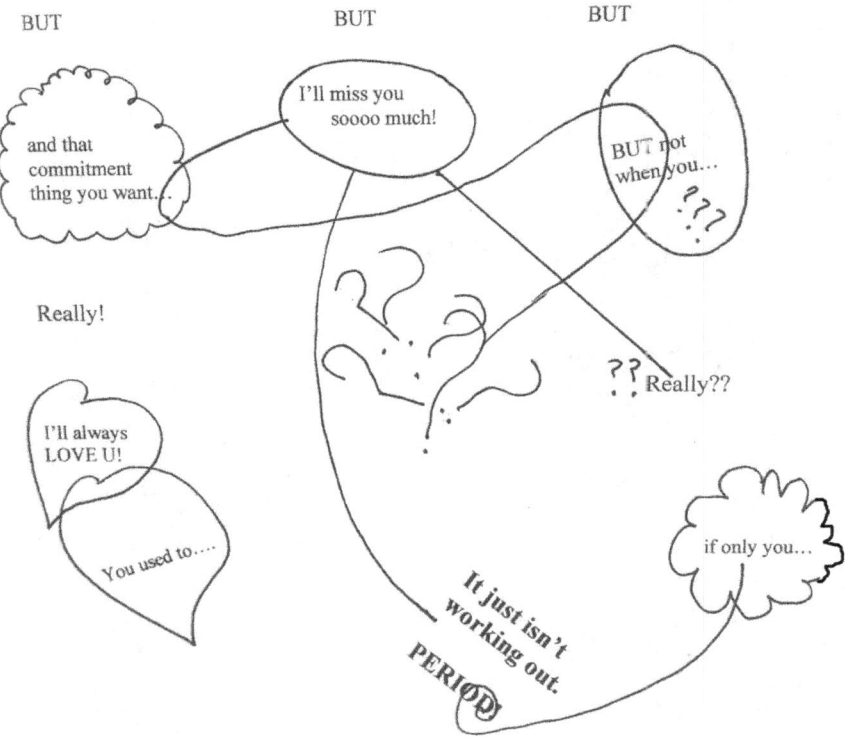

In Words of One Syllable

I hate your guts.

  (I love you)

I wish I were dead.

  (SAVE ME!)

Shut up! Screw you! Fuck off!

(Don't leave me!!)

Unspoken

I love you so much (……………….)

but I'm drinking my coffee, tweeting, napping, watching a Netflix, screwing, facebooking, fixing the toilet, watching porn, texting my girlfriendboyfriendbffbossdealer…………………………………………so

                                                        skidoo
                                      go fly a kite
bug off
              beat it   drop dead
      scram   get lost
                                take a hike   buzz off
       shove off
                go play in traffic
get moving
     go jump in the lake take a walk climb a tree go fuck a duck

Pick your poison, but

Get Lost

Before (The) After
(Quaker Meeting)

In memory of Chuck Woodbury, 1922-2018

        Quiet.

        Door open. Bird sings.

        Quiet.

        Bird sings. Tree

        sways. Breeze

        bends branches.

Quiet.

You rise.

        Consider the leaf,

        you say, that's blown

        through the door. Like

        the spirit, free to come in.

        You sit.

        Quiet.

Quieter.

Mobile

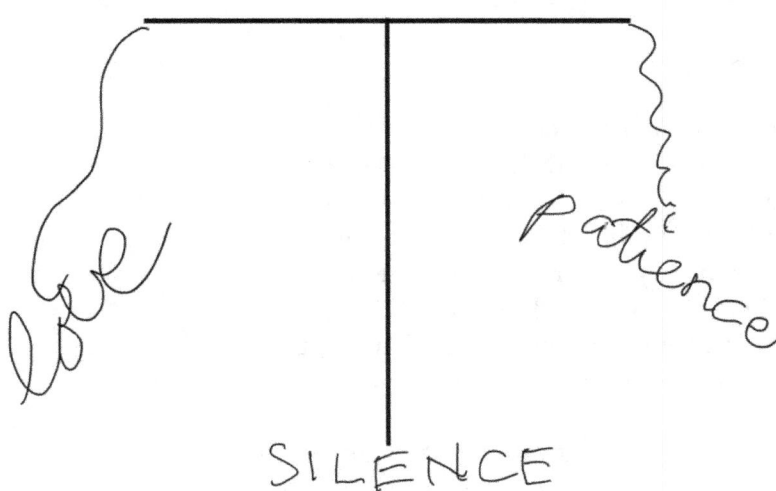

Christmas Oratorio

House quiet

No one home

It's our time at last, sings Refrigerator,
a baritone. Clock adds her gentle castanet.
Light Bulb takes up his drone. Mischievous
Wind picks up her flute. A playful trill, while
Raindrop taps a metronome on the patio.
Oil Burner growls its deep ground bass.
Computer enters on middle C, delivering an email.
iphone echoes him an octave higher.

Wait! Is that a child calling from the sidewalk?

A New Song

Excuse me—
      What's that song you're singing?
      You're making it up? As you sing?
      May I join you?   Of course—
      don't worry—it will be my own song,
      my own tune, my own words
      or not-words—perhaps a nigun—oh

Did you say you'd like to make a song together?
      Yes? YES!

      A new song for a new day. All the new days.
      All the new songs. A prayer book to believe in.

And you too?

      You do?

Please Submit a Brief Bio

I have a who singing silently to your who singing
silently to my who, whoever and whomever
knows how to love, whose mouth knows how to kiss to make
words leap like ballerinas, glide like kayaks in white
water, high tide breathless fast paddling
fast swimming in swift currents, jet-skiing hang-
gliding syllables words sentences type-
faces strange and stranger, other languages, symbols
characters libraries and on-line dictionaries
waving tildes, diaereses, circumflexes, and
the sexy ç-cedillas, pictures imported and ex-
ported up/downloaded ballads anthems carols
fugues lullabies etudes concertos symphonies
marches chants arias sung played my inner
orchestra my instruments of long ago and now
every bagpipe, saxophone 'cello lute maracas
viola flute harp and trumpet piccolo bassoon.
My erhu. My pipa. My simple rain-
stick. My Biblical ram's horn all now all then
all when my who which wants wants wants to be
here (and there) when the world is and was and will
be beyond time and space, beyond you, beyond
beyond, and   beyond.

Calling

my dream dreams on in its dreamlogic   cows
are turning into people *cower*   *coward*   people
long dead are young again in countries their hungry
eyes have never seen   no man (woman) is *an island*
an is-land *an eye-land*   *an I-land*   I wander the
landscape   sadness dusts the leaves my old friend Ferdinand
ambles by smelling the flowers   a *llama* led by a brain-
damaged girl lopes by my house   I am reminded
of a Lama's practice of Tonglen *breathe in the pain*
of the world   *your pain is my pain*   *breathe out*
compassion   *for you*   *for me*   *for you*
       for me

I hear you calling me   far away but clear   clear
zen gongs   the dingdong of your iv apparatus   my
name   *marian, marian*   *in your sleep, in*
my sleep.

Spring Sunlight

Green leaves growing
Photograph fading

Hair greying
Forsythia yellowing

Turtles mating
Candlestick tarnishing

Sparrow waking
me. You sleeping.

Synesthesia

spirals of dream   and
photograph of symphony
painting of sonnet   sand
poem of singing star
dancing out-breath   frozen
fossil flame   moon-
branch   etched
stave of Arctic stone   in
Agra, in Angkor Wat,
in Isfahan, in   your timeless   hand

Auld Lang Syne

This just might be

Today might be

Never forget
seize
kiss
wrap
Because
be the same as
what

will never
is, which is
was

Deciding

I WILL (not?) DO IT!
I w~~ill~~ (might) not do it...

But if I might do it (if...?)
& I do it to help me?
Isn't there some rule...?

WHAT would my mother say!
Can't anyone ???

Cartography

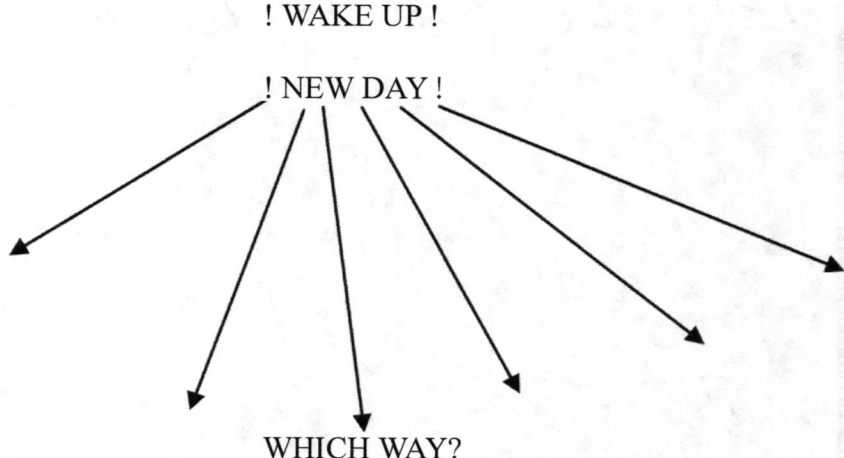

"If Not Now, When?"

Hillel

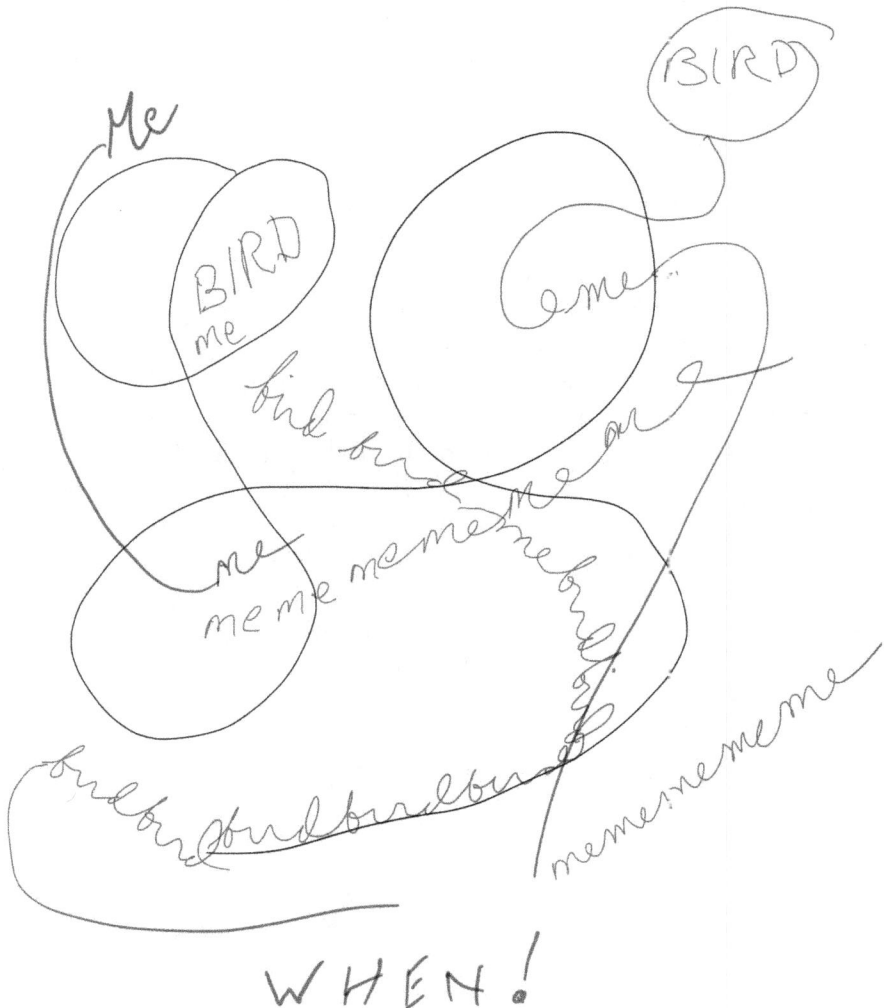

Pure Love

To my grandfather, Edward (Isaak) Kaplun,
b. 18 April, 1880. d. 31 May, 1955

                your love   flies
            across the   centuries
                on the backs of camels
                      and whales   your
        letters   dance, spin strong with   the
swirls   of your oldfashioned handwriting   elegant
           windswept sssssssssss's, caterpillars of
mmmmmmmmm's and nnnnnnnnnnnn's, gaggles of ggggggggs
      and pppppppppppp's, stanchions of lllllllllllllllllllllll's,
              portholes of ooooooooooooo's
                   constellations of   stellar
              specks ballooning   skyward
set free from   i's   and   j's
           on the other side of the invisible world
              where we are both perfect,
                    where you live

   and where you love me from

Non-Sense

There's nothing to say about the green
that hasn't been said before about the red the blue the yellow wall-
paper peppered with cornflowers, the raspberries on the counter
the coffee grinder set to espresso, the cabinets that whisperclose
themselves sighing graciously on the cupsmugsglasses resting
on their hooks and racks, the drawers of cookbooks, mildewed
manuals, and long expired coupons, the knives of special shapes and
sizes for the cuttingslicingdicing of the carrots celery mushrooms
onions breads and (yes) the meats; the closet for the brooms the
brushes sponges, brillo, all the soapspowders for the cleaningshining
of the pots and plates and bowls and un-silverware, and what to
say about the pre-smart fridge that cannot clean itself, or learn to
scan the sell-by dates, issuing pithy action orders (toss the milk),
channeling her twin sister Our Lady of the GPS (turn left on Main),
there's nothing to say at all about the kitchen
except that I love that you like your morning coffee
in the Eiffel tower mug.

Editing It Down

[handwritten margin notes: "simplify / unnecessary" and "rhythm"]

What's worth saying? ~~Hasn't it all been said before? And,~~ what ~~good has any of the saying done? Words and words and words.~~ About Peace. Love. Justice. ~~About War.~~ Murder. ~~Torture. What we want. How much~~ we hope against hope. ~~How~~ we love, and lose, and love again.

One way or another

it will happen
because we are alive.
We animals.
We fish. We birds.
We plants.
              Or,
it will happen
whether or not.

Stone. Mountain. Star.

'Across the Miles'

(reflections on a Hallmark card)

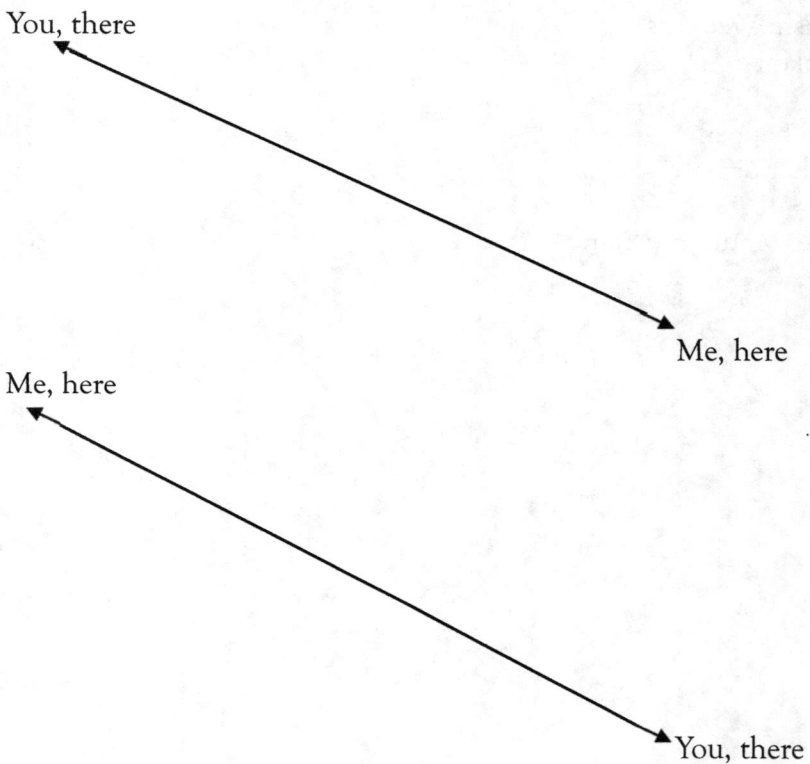

The measure the same.
The distance different.

Breakfast, Together

flavor of star
color of air
shape of shimmer

bowl   bowl
cup   cup
spoon   spoon

texture of
unsaid,
sound of

are

Wind Advisory

                    The trees are talking to each other

hmmm   *hmmm*

(*the ones with leaves*   (the ones without leaves
the ones with leaves to lose)   the ones whose leaves are lost)

Nothing to do but wait.
                This is how it happened.
Nothing to do but worry.
                Colors came brilliant sparking
questions. Who will fall?
                like candles, bright sputterings
and when will they fall? And
                before the final breath.
will I bear the falling? And
                you won't, you can't get used to
the emptiness. The missing
                it. They say in Spring

Nothing will be the same.
                buds will grow, flowers and
Surrender. No one to blame.
                fruit will follow. You don't feel better.

Loss is loss.   Loss is loss.
The wind is the wind.   The wind is the wind.

                *hmmm*hmmm
                    hmmm*hmmm*

Modern Haiku (while aggravated)

Rate this poem:

Helpful? ☑

Unhelpful? ☑

Inappropriate? ☑

Make up your fu'n mind!

Getting to the Point

~~A point. A dot. The end of a sentence. The main idea, that took someone too long to get to. As in~~

~~*The point is....* The end of the discussion, like it or not. As in *That's the way it is:*~~

Period.

Fauré Requiem: Les Fenêtres de Ste Chapelle, 18h30

                      strawberries

      cerises   poire caramel

mirabelle   essence de lime

     citron   candied orange

           cherries   rouge   bleu

et rose   jaune

           (*la lumière de la lumière*)   (*light*

of lights)   (*perpetual*   *and eternal light unto us*)

   green   pommes   et   mangue

     sucre   vapeur de

   meringue naturel   fraîche

abricot   plums

        en vin rouge, en

  vin blanc   white

peach   arome de

     pear

            fraises

Sing to me in sorbet d'orange

en grand marnier

(*lux perpetua, lux aeterna*

luceat eis; lumière à nous,

lumen de lumine

lumière née de la lumière)

before the sun sets.

Living Together

eating working walking reading driving making dinner, making love making babies growing them up waving goodbyes. Have a good time! Come home early, don't (whatever), drive carefully, keep well, see you at Thanksgiving, bye, bye, bye, bye....

The pines of Maine are swaying in their summer dance. Calypso's thrumming from the blueberry bushes (1960) or is it Fado (1988) Tango (2000) rhumba (1955) cha cha (1957) meringue (1976) whose limbs are these entangled with each other on which beds in which cities soft young skin smooth unscarred but for a few reminders of roller skating bike riding bungee jumping, dreams ambitions fears what used to be so very life or death important grades approval (disapproval) the all-significant red pen, the (god forbid) thin envelope the phone that wouldn't wouldn't (!) ring, the letter signed best instead of love....

Suburban Back Yard

                              Instead of chickadees
                                                              and
                                       squirrels
            and   robins,   sparrows,

chipmunks   or
                  a

                      visiting groundhog,   even a red fox or   a
thin   grey

            wolf   come down from the hills   looking for

water in a season of drought,

                                       I wake

to a full-grown African elephant, keeping company with a lioness,
one very black bear, a spindly giraffe, a Bengal tiger, a snow leopard,
its paw resting on the shoulder of its neighbor hyena, and a jaguar
napping in the shade of our tallest oak tree. A lynx is cavorting with
a cheetah over by the tulip bed, a monkey hanging upside-down
from the roof, and a chimpanzee rocking contentedly under the
swingset, near the day-lilies. A coral snake is sunning on a nearby
rock, a beaded necklace of red and gold. When I point excitedly out
the kitchen window, my anonymous house-guests, pouring second
cups of coffee, nod pleasantly, but observe that the sugar bowl is
empty and the silver tongs are nowhere to be seen.

Before the Memorial Day Weekend

Friday
    Hot. Humid.

Turnpike boiling with traffic. A volley of horns. A shootout of curses.

      (*F-ing orange cones*)
            (*goddamned if I'll let that gonif in*)

Why not take the country bypass.
      Farmstands. Corn. Strawberries. Pie.
      Century-old houses with gambrel roofs. One
      school bus, lights flashing. Two bicycles. And

—sheep! Black, white, brown, all fat, curly-wooled, ambling with their lambs in a surprise of long grassy pasture. Seemingly comfortable, despite their winter coats. Encased within the auto glass, I am a shepherd sealed in air-conditioned sunlight, where humidity doesn't'count. Thinking *I'm a lucky woman and I want to stay that way.*

Saturday
    Hot. Humid.

Turnpike quiet.
Revelers at their barbecues.
Still,

      I choose the bypass for an-
      other dose of peace.

The field was empty.
But my Friday eyes saw sheep.
Lambs. Do you see them?

Pain. Hope.

Thanks be

for the space between

the bombs (~ ~ ~ ~ ~ ~ ~)the rockets (~ ~)

the lances (~ ~ ~ ~ ~ ~ ~ ~) the daggers (~ ~) the swords (~ ~) the knives (~ ~)

the axes (~ ~ ~ ~ ~ ~ ~ ~ ~ ~ ~ ~ ~ ~) the fires (~ ~ ~ ~ ~ ~ ~ ~ ~ ~ ~ ~ ~ ~)

the bludgeons (~ ~ ~ ~) the hatchets (~ ~ ~ ~) the spears, the bayonets (~ ~ ~ ~)

And (~ ~) always the guns. From bb's to

blunderbusses.   From screams to moans.

Your afternoon was atom-bombed to dust. The Cruelest of the Cruel crushed your stash of Percoset with a tire iron. The air scintillates with blood, fresh and dried. Bruises. Burns. Cuts and blisters. Puncture wounds. Nausea.

That was yesterday. And the week/s before.

Today, however, is the Day of the Space Between. This morning you can walk to town. Coffee with a friend. A hug goodbye. Meander home, stopping for fruit at the farmer's market. An hour with a book in your favorite chair; for writing in your notebook or your laptop.

Hope, that 'thing with feathers' rises like fresh dough.
I pray you know, and never have to know. That space
that keeps you waking up, day after day. Not dead.
Not wishing to be dead. Thanks be.

Learning from Bees

    (in Rangeley, Maine)

Someone's sunning on the dock
chanting. *Om mani padme Hum.*
Om mani padme Hum. I'm
having an affair with shade from
the old birch tree, moving my pen
to the rhythm of the whitecaps, topped
off by a motor boat far upshore.
A loon calls out. Is answered. Calls.
Is answered. Crow caws. Gull screams.
Cardinal inserts its 6-note song. Leaves
whisk the air, like beaters in a bowl
of sweet whipped cream. Shouts of children
from the cabin. Happy. Full of school's
out and soft-serve.

                Can you taste
the chocolate cone? the anadama bread?
the cherry pies? Do you miss the way
the full moon coyly slides between the clouds,
romancing its image mirrored in the lake?
Do you hear the world of silence made
of lapping waves?

             The bees are lighting
on all sides of me.
Back home, I maintain the DMZ.
Here the bees and I forget to worry.
Here, I neglect to lock my car.

Om mani padme Hum. Om
mani padme Hum.. .The bees are burring
softly. Softly. I'm getting the hang
of living like they do,
of living like this.

Echolalia, in September

leaves falling   leaves of fall falling   fall falling   leaves leaving
berries burying   when roses rose (the last rose of summer) some
of her   floated into perfume   few per-many per-men-y   so few
permanent so many gone

Bereavement Group

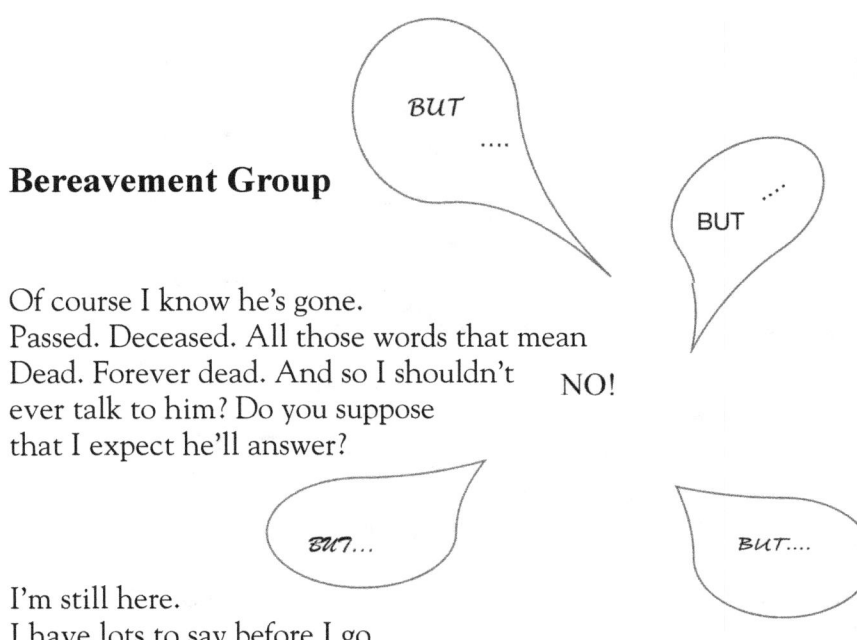

Of course I know he's gone.
Passed. Deceased. All those words that mean
Dead. Forever dead. And so I shouldn't
ever talk to him? Do you suppose
that I expect he'll answer?

I'm still here.
I have lots to say before I go
wherever that may be
(or may not be).
Aren't the widowed loons still calling?
the lonely dogs still barking? If only to themselves?
Like humming, singing, whistling, once it's gotten going
it's on its way, rolling down the slope
on its own schedule.

Blow softly, wind.
Rock gently, hammock.
Sway, birch.
Swing low, sweet chariot.
Play me a lullaby. The one I need.

Internet Search

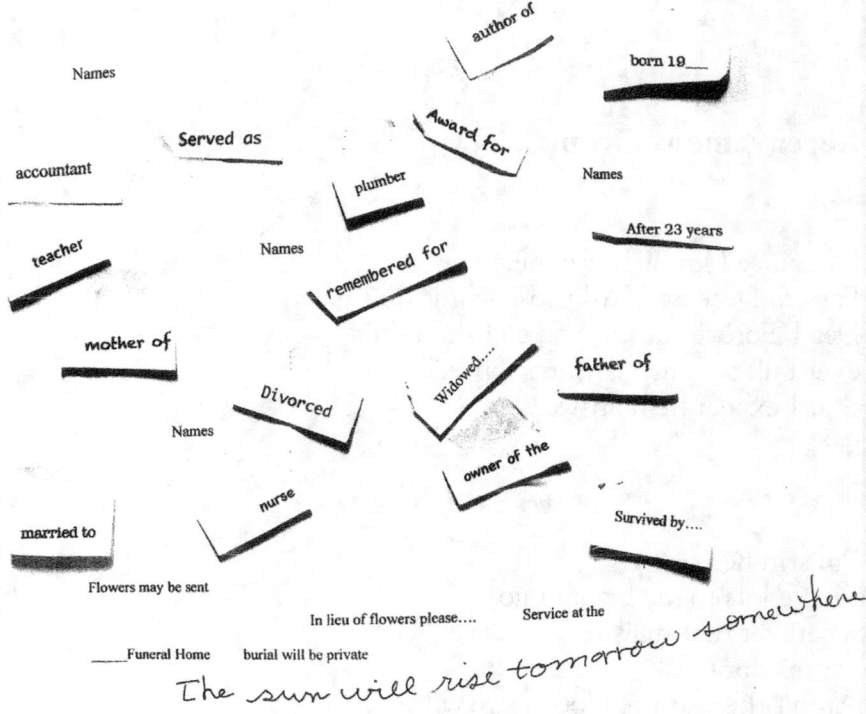

Equation: A Conversation

...
+
~ - :
= ?

!
-
< > +/- (?) =
...

?
-
* @ [ ] =
(∞) ...

Weathering the War of Words

<u>Storm</u>

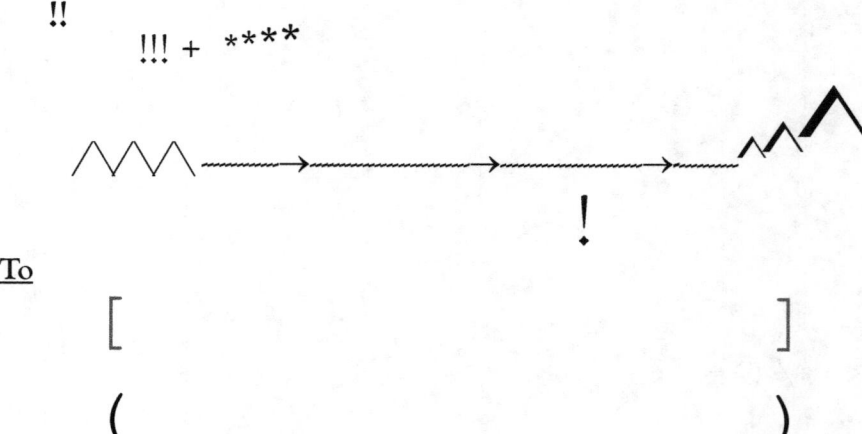

<u>To</u>

[ ]
( )

<u>Calm</u>

....
.............................?

?..............#............#...............#..

mmmmmmmm.......

mmmmmmmmmm.......

Communication

Why   you   yesterday? she says loudly, from the kitchen.

                saying? he answers, from the bedroom.

       to decide today,   you   ?

What? Can't

Why don't you just come in here so you can hear me!

Why don't YOU come in HERE!

Hearing/Not Hearing in the Conference Hall

                                                                                smoke

wisp

Would you please speak a little louder?
Sure, sorry, **I was saying that** it is very important to **consider** the impact such decisions will make .....

                                                                              mist

Static   *fizz*

              coughing   *firecrackers*

                  Flies   chimes   ;'s

                      Laughing < laughing < **laughing** <
(?)   :

Puffballs (to wish on)   (...

      weeping

                                  doves
                                               on the window sill

              kites let go of

)

Anxious Attachment

Find me the heart of the matter
the center around which the planets spin
around which we orbit our tenuous stay
on earth, our fierce tether to each other
whipped by invisible winds,
twisters attacking with only moments warning,
gyrating frantically   from love
to desperation   from desperation
to love

Assembly

This

                                                                                         we

            Hungry

how

    is   we   *we*

,

                                                                 how

Ever

                  live

for

how

                                                                  we

,   *how*   **hungry**

feel   .   .

                                                                                 wait

love   think

After finishing a meal, we Americans may say, "I'm full."
En France nous disons "Ça suffit."

Neither is true.

This is how we think, how we live, how we feel, how we wait for love.
Hungry. Ever hungry.

Right Triangles

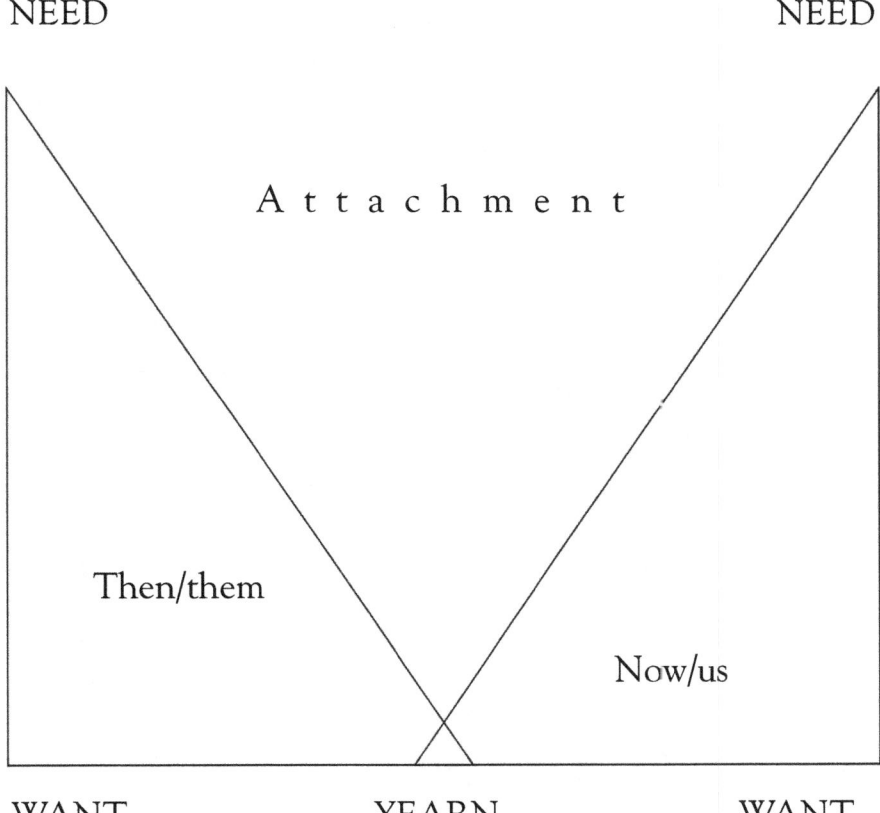

Behind You There Is Nothing[*]

Embrace it.

---

[*] *Always in writing at the back of words are no words, behind you is nothing. That nothing holds us up. Embrace it."* —from article by Natalie Goldberg, "Wild At Heart" (pp. 28-31) in *Five Points*, **12:1**, 2008, was excerpted from her book, *Old Friend From Far Away*.

Around here, March

would give anything for lovesongs of
wild roses on the window sill.
A Carmen kind of red. Blazing.
Defiant. Aflame with desire.

        My skin,
              pale and dry,
                  dreams   sun on grass,
            dreams dew
                 turned to sparkling stars
                     fallen
                           from the sky
                 while we
                       were sleeping.

                           Spring!
                             Spring!

                      it sings.

        But the sun
has its own itinerary. Its own
timetable. Immutable. In your body,

        in
            every cell
                your genes turn on, alive
           silent
              stalks of waiting

      for the light. Somewhere in this world

the sun is playing castanets. Habaneras hot enough to make March shout for joy, twirl impassioned tangos, seductive double dips of lust and longing.

Somewhere in this world
the spirit is moving

reminding me that it is present,

                invisible

                                (*visibilium et invisibilium*)

                                      possibile (et impossibile)

to count on.

Life Lessons

Watch your back
Mind your own business
Don't talk to strangers
Better safe than sorry
Shoot first, ask questions later
Everyone's out for themselves
Look out for #1

love, respect, lovers, friends, peace, bed, joy

Experiments in

sound of space, silence
        of words   rhythm
             of freedom

the shock

of discovering what you have always (almost) known

You place your precious life on black velvet

    Yesterday, a brilliant diamond. Radiant. Fierce. Brave. Bold.

       Today, an incandescent pearl, glowing softly, spirit singing.

Climbing

(from the ground up)

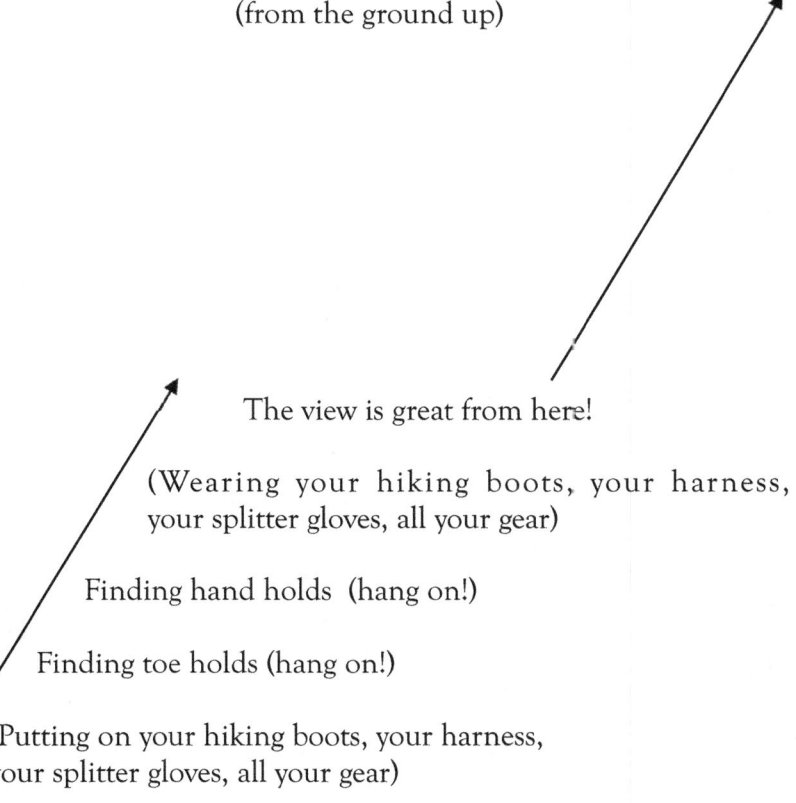

The view is great from here!

(Wearing your hiking boots, your harness, your splitter gloves, all your gear)

Finding hand holds (hang on!)

Finding toe holds (hang on!)

(Putting on your hiking boots, your harness, your splitter gloves, all your gear)

The view will be great from there.

Acknowledgements

Gratitude to publications who have previously published these poems:

Part 1:
"What We Know", *Free State Review*, Jan 2020; "Over Your Head", *American Writers Review*, 2019; "Plane Geometry", *Maximum Tilt Anthology*, 2019; "Summer's", *Gyroscope*, 2015; and *Celestial Musings Anthology*, 2018; "John Cage In The Wild", *Cyclamens and Swords*, Aug 2010; "Blow Up", *Talking Writing*, 2015-2016; "Clocks" (in a different form), *Festival Writer*, June 2014; "3 a.m", *Third Wednesday*, 2014; "Stonehenge", *Miranda*, 2006; "Gardening", *Poetry Quarterly*, 2016; "Tree/Winter", *RiverSedge*, 2018; "Bird Calls", *Bacopa*, 2010

Part 2:
"Memoir", *Capable*, Feb 2020; "Rape", California Writers Association, First Prize in *Homestead Magazine*, 2012; and *Cahoodaloodaling*, 2016; "Dividing Line", *MER*, Dec. 2015; and *ArtAscent*, April 2016; "You're Still Hung Up", *New Delta Review*, 2012; and *Long Island Literary Journal*, 2017; "Wednesday, During The Hurricane", *Crosswinds*, 2016; and *Loon Magic Anthology*, 2019; "Late Night Flight", *Main Channel*, 2005; and *Maximum Tilt Anthology*, 2020; "Instructions To Child Victims", *Tusculum*, Feb., 2005; *Interrobang*, 2010; and *Loose Moose Anthology*, 2016; "Mayday", *Homestead Review*, 2006; "Internal Monologue", *Hamline*, 2019

Part 3:
"Empathy", *Capable*, Feb 2020; "Monkey Mind," *Inquiring Mind*, Fall, 2006; and Shapiro, *Players In The Dream, Dreamers In The Play*, 2007; "Before (The) After", *Sufi Journal*, Summer 2012; *Journal of Modern Poetry*, 2018; *Types and Shadows*, 2016; and *New York Quarterly Anthology: Without A Doubt*, 2021; "Mobile", Shapiro, *Players In The Dream, Dreamers In The Play*, 2007; "Christmas Oratorio", *Poetry Quarterly*, Dec 2015; "Please Submit A Brief Bio", *Literal Latte*, 2009; and *Journal of Modern Poetry*, 2013; "Calling", *Pebble Lake*, Winter, 2004; *Laughing Gull* Contest (1st prize) 2005; Shapiro, *Parenthesis*, 2005; Senior Poet Laureate of Massachusetts 2006; and Shapiro, *Players In The Dream, Dreamers In The Play*, 2007; "Spring Sunlight", *DuPage Review*, 2009;

Modern Poetry Review, 2012; and *Types and Shadows*, 2019; "Synesthesia", *Promise*, 2004; and Shapiro, *Players In The Dream, Dreamers In The Play*, 2007; "Auld Lang Syne", *Calamus*, 2016; "Ellipses," Shapiro, *Players In The Dream, Dreamers In The Play*, 2007; "Cartography", *Silver Pinyon*, 2019; "Pure Love" , *Wild Goose*, Spring, 2006; and Shapiro, *Players In The Dream, Dreamers In The Play*, 2007; "Non-Sense", *Bacopa* 2017; "Editing It Down," *Common Ground*, 2008; "Breakfast, Together", *Tethered By Letters*, 2014; "Fauré Requiem", *Du Page Review*, 2009; and *ArtAscent*, 2017; "Quaker Meeting On The Concord River", *Types and Shadows*, 2008; "Living Together", *Talking Writing*, 2016; "Suburban BackYard", *Tigers Eye*, Spring, 2006; "Before The Memorial Day Weekend", *Bacopa*, June 2017; "Learning From Bees", *NLAPA Portland* 2010; *Bacopa* 2011; and *The Nature Of Things Anthology* 2012; "Echolalia", *New Delta Review*, 2012; "Internet Search", *Inverted Syntax*, Aug 2018; "Equation", *Maximum Tilt Anthology*, 2019; and *Silver Pinion*, 2019; "Hearing/Not Hearing", *Passager*, June 2019; "Right Triangles", *Capable*, Feb., 2020; "In Words Of One Syllable", *Cahaba*, 2015; "Cryopediology", *Verseweavers* (2nd prize), 2015; "Behind You There Is Nothing", *Shadowgraph*, Jan 2014; "Around here, March," *The Quotable*, Feb 2013; and *ArtAscent*, Dec 2015; "Life Lessons;" *Types and Shadows*, Spring 2020; "Speaking Up", *Types and Shadows*, Spring 2020

About the Author

Photo by Steven Shapiro

    Having grown up in a housing project in The Bronx, Marian Kaplun Shapiro is delighted to be practicing as a psychologist from her home office in Lexington, Massachusetts, looking out on woods, flowers, birds, and unpolluted sky. She attended the then free Queens College, where she received her B.A. in English with a minor in music, and studied writing with Stanley Kunitz and Stephen Stepanchev. At 20 she married her astrophysicist husband and attended Harvard for a Masters in Teaching and English, studying poetry writing with Archibald MacLeish.

    Teaching, two children, teaching again and then a return to Harvard for a doctorate in Psychology, culminated in a private practice as a psychologist, which she still pursues. In her forties she returned to writing: first, a professional book, next articles and chapters in psychology textbooks, and then a deep dive into poetry, resulting in approximately 450 publications, one book (*Players In The Dream, Dreamers In The Play*, Plain View Press 2007), and two chapbooks. Working with victims of violence, she recognized that in her heart she was a Quaker, and joined the Society of Friends, which holds an important place in her life and poetry. Now over 80, she is fortunate in loving and being loved by her adoring and adored husband, adult children, their spouses, and their five kind, funny, smart, talented, delightful children. Life to her is one long experiment, and she is unendingly grateful that hers has turned out so amazingly well.

www.ingramcontent.com/pod-product-compliance
Lightning Source LLC
Chambersburg PA
CBHW071642080526
44586CB00013BA/1341